# Eleanor Roosevelt

## First Lady of the World

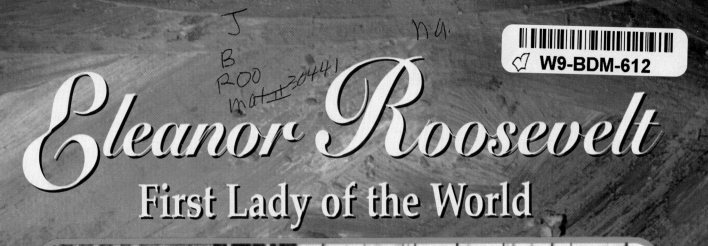

*"You must do the thing you think you cannot do."*

# Early Years

Eleanor Roosevelt was born in New York City on October 11, 1884. Eleanor was not a happy child. She was plain and shy, and she spent much of her time alone or with servants.

Eleanor (second from right) with her father and brothers

Eleanor's parents had died by the time she was ten years old. She and her brother lived with their grandmother, who had many strict rules.

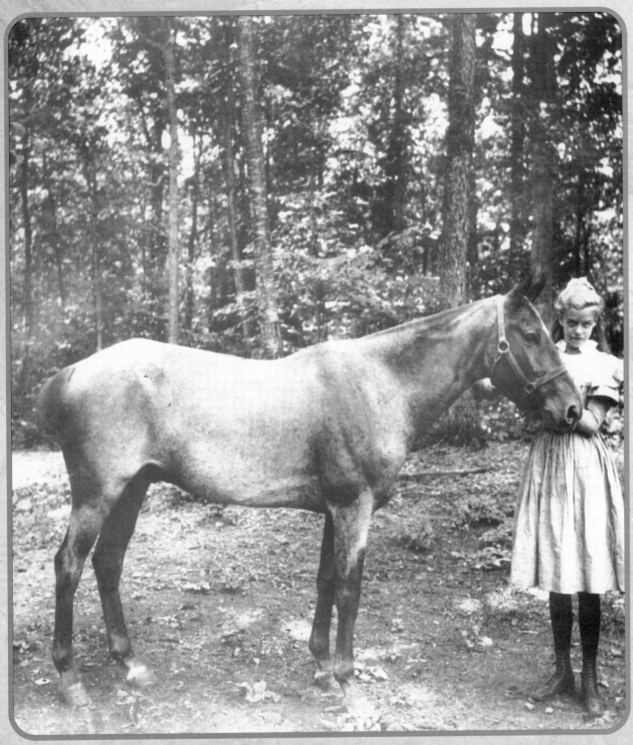

Eleanor was fond of horses, but not of long stockings and high shoes.

# At School

Eleanor was sent away to school in England. For the first time, she had friends. Eleanor discovered how exciting learning could be and that helping others was important.

Eleanor
at fifteen

Eleanor returned to New York
when she was eighteen.
She began to spend time
with a distant cousin,
Franklin Delano
Roosevelt. They fell in
love and were
married.

The Roosevelt family

While Franklin was at work, Eleanor cared for her large family. She was surrounded by baby nurses and servants to help her.

Eleanor and her children

# Eleanor the Leader

When Franklin went to work in government, Eleanor's life changed. She was interested in meeting and talking with many different people.

Eleanor became a newswoman.

Eleanor traveled all over America and the world. Here she is about to enter a coal mine.

7

When Franklin was elected president of the United States, Eleanor became the First Lady. Both Eleanor and Franklin believed that government should help people in need.

Franklin D. Roosevelt

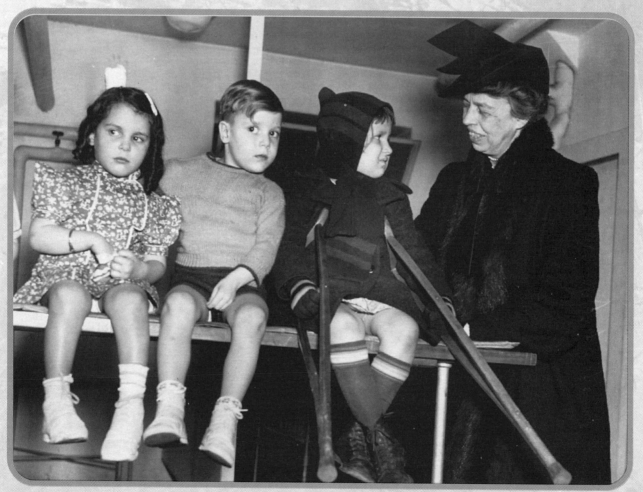

Eleanor cared about people. Here she visits children at a hospital.

Eleanor had the courage to stand up for what she believed. The Daughters of the American Revolution would not allow Marian Anderson, a great singer, to perform in their concert hall because she was African American. Eleanor gave up her membership in the group in protest.

Eleanor invited Marian Anderson to sing in front of the Lincoln Memorial.

On December 7, 1941, the United States entered the Second World War. Eleanor traveled around the world to visit American soldiers.

Eleanor visiting a United States aircraft carrier

After Franklin's death, Eleanor became part of the United States group at the United Nations. There she worked with other leaders for peace.

Eleanor is shown here answering news reporters' questions.

n.a.

Eleanor was a strong speaker, and she wrote a daily newspaper article. She was admired by people around the world.

Eleanor died on November 7, 1962 at the age of seventy-eight. At her funeral, President Harry S. Truman called her "First Lady of the World."

This photo was taken the year before Eleanor died.

# Let's Explore!

Hyde Park, the home of the Roosevelts, is now a national park. What are some of the places to visit there?

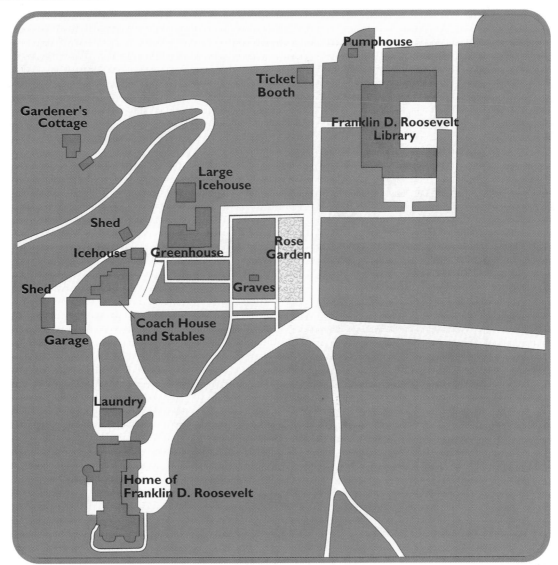

The Roosevelt home, Hyde Park, New York

13

# What Do You Think?

## How I Help Others

Eleanor helped many people. List ways you help others. Then use your list to write a story about helping someone. Share your story.

### A Poem for Eleanor

Write a poem telling why you think Eleanor was such a special person. Draw a picture for your poem.

## MAKE A POSTER

Eleanor worked so that people had good jobs. Draw or paint a poster. Tell why you want good jobs for everyone.

# OTHER FIRST LADIES

**Jacqueline Kennedy Onassis** won praise for making the White House a historic showplace for visiting dignitaries and tourists alike.

**Lady Bird Johnson** won recognition for sponsoring projects aimed at the beautification of interstate highways and the District of Columbia.

**Nancy Reagan** sponsored activities that targeted drug and alcohol abuse in young people, becoming famous for her "Just say no!" to drugs campaign.

**Barbara Bush** understood the importance of learning to read and helped start the Barbara Bush Foundation for Family Literacy.

# Key Events

| | |
|---|---|
| **1884** | **Born in New York City on October 11** |
| **1899** | **Sent to school in England** |
| **1905** | **Married Franklin Delano Roosevelt** |
| **1933-1945** | **Was First Lady of the United States** |
| **1942** | **Visited soldiers during the war** |
| **1945** | **Appointed to the United Nations** |
| **1962** | **Died on November 7** |

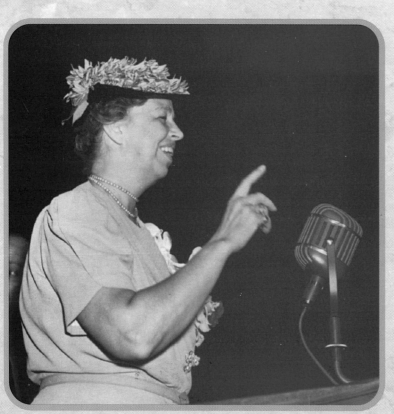

At the 1940
Democratic Convention